Quilted Projects for a
Country Christmas

Quilted Projects for a
Country Christmas

Connie Duran

Sterling Publishing Co., Inc.
New York

Chapelle, Ltd.:
Jo Packham
Sara Toliver
Cindy Stoeckl

Library of Congress Cataloging-in-Publication Data
Duran, Connie.
  Quilted projects for a country Christmas / Connie Duran.
    p. cm.
  "A Sterling/Chapelle Book."
  Includes index.
  ISBN 1-4027-1155-7
  1. Patchwork--Patterns. 2. Quilting. 3. Christmas decorations. I.
Title.

TT835.D885 2004
746.46--dc22

                                          2004016644

10 9 8 7 6 5 4 3 2 1

Published in paperback in 2006 by Sterling Publishing Co., Inc.
387 Park Avenue South, New York, NY 10016
© 2004 by Connie Duran
Distributed in Canada by Sterling Publishing
c/o Canadian Manda Group, 165 Dufferin Street
Toronto, Ontario, Canada M6K 3H6
Distributed in Great Britain by GMC Distribution Services,
Castle Place, 166 High Street, Lewes, East Sussex, England BN7 1XU
Distributed in Australia by Capricorn Link (Australia) Pty. Ltd.
P. O. Box 704, Windsor, NSW 2756, Australia
Printed and Bound in China
All Rights Reserved

Sterling ISBN-13: 978-1-4027-1155-8 Hardcover
        ISBN-10: 1-4027-1155-7

        ISBN-13: 978-1-4027-4067-1 Paperback
        ISBN-10: 1-4027-4067-0

For information about custom editions, special sales, premium
and corporate purchases, please contact Sterling Special Sales
Department at 800-805-5489 or specialsales@sterlingpub.com.

TABLE OF CONTENTS

Warming Up the Hearth

16

36

Spicy Delight

Cozy Corners

50

78

Elegant Touches

PREFACE

This book was created for those who love to quilt for the holidays, who want to create something made by hand for family and friends, and who yearn for a special link to the less complicated days of Christmases long past. This is a book wherein the patterns are familiar yet new, and which can be easily re-created with the push of a photocopier button. The step-by-step instructions take you from the selection of fabrics to the completion of the handwork, and do so in detailed uncomplicated steps.

Each project, photographed in a Christmas setting that gives ideas for Christmas decorating, also includes additional quilt block patterns for a second and a third project to create a "set" or multiple gifts for holiday giving. In addition to the quilt ideas, I show you how to make several of the projects from paper. The combination of paper, buttons, and fibers is a new "idea" for traditional fabric decorations and offers a new technique for the traditional quilter.

GENERAL INSTRUCTIONS

How to Use This Book

Before beginning the projects, familiarize yourself with the book. A general supply list and overall instructions are provided in this chapter. The list includes tools and items to keep on hand while doing the projects. The instructions cover techniques on using patterns, tea-dyeing fabrics, antiquing tags and cardstock, and stitching with flosses.

With every project, a specific supply list is given along with step-by-step instructions. A full-page project photograph is shown as a guide to adding the finishing touches.

In addition to the featured projects, optional quilt patterns are given, some shown with a "tag" of explanation. These can be used to replace one of the blocks in the featured project, or to spark ideas for new projects. Though they are not explained in a stepped-out manner, the blocks can be made using the same techniques as other similar pieces throughout the book.

Patterns for the featured projects are found in the back of the book. We have also included some additional patterns and artwork that you can use to create your own unique pieces. The patterns and artwork can be reduced or enlarged on a color or black-and-white photocopier based on your specific needs.

Dyeing Techniques

Using Walnut Ink Crystals

This product is great for antiquing papers. Simply mix the powder-like crystals with water according to the instructions on the package. Pour the solution into a spray bottle. Spray on paper edges to give a little bit of a worn look. Or, place the solution in a bowl to soak shipping tags and cardstock to desired shade. Lay flat on a towel or hang to drip dry. The wet paper may wrinkle on the corners and edges, but the effect can be desirable. Control the wrinkling by placing a heavy object on it while drying or by using an iron with the aid of a towel until the paper dries. Either method requires the paper item to be fully dry upon completion. *Note: If the desired shade of antiquing is not achieved, the dyeing process can be repeated.*

Using Tea

Muslin is the most commonly used fabric when tea dyeing. When applying tea dye to fabrics, do not put light-colored fabrics and dark-colored fabrics together. Place 6–7 tablespoons of instant tea or approximately six tablespoons of instant coffee into a large kettle filled with water. Heat over medium temperature until mixture is hot, but not boiling.

Remove from heat. Immerse fabric in tea-dye mixture and soak for at least 30 minutes. When fabric has been dyed to desired color, remove from mixture and wring out. When possible, hang fabric to air-dry; this will make the hue darker.

To tea-dye an entire quilt block once it has been completed, place the tea-dye mixture into a spray bottle. Spray the project in a sink or dish to avoid overspray. Allow fabric to air-dry.

General Supplies

Keeping the basic tools and materials on hand while doing the projects from this book will streamline completion. Here are the suggested items:

- Adhesives: clear dots, craft glue, double-sided artist's tape, fabric glue, glue stick, hot-glue gun

- Black fine-tipped permanent marker

- Craft wires, assorted gauges

- Disappearing fabric-ink pen

- Embroidery flosses

- Embroidery hoops

- Embroidery needles

- Fabric-marking pencils: dark, light

- Fusible webbing

- Iron and ironing board

- Light source: computer monitor, light-box, television, window

- Matching threads

- Paper/cotton towels

- Pencil

- Photocopier

- Rotary cutter

- Ruler

- Scissors: craft, fabric

- Scrapbook papers

- Scraps: fabric, felt, lace, ribbon, trims

- Self-healing cutting mat

- Sewing machine

- Sewing needles

- Sponge brushes

- Straight pins

- Tape measure

- Tea-dye mixture

- Walnut ink crystals

Using Patterns

Photocopy and place patterns pertaining to individual project pieces and instructions. For pattern pieces, place fabric on flat work surface and use an appropriate colored fabric-marking pencil to trace around cut-out patterns.

When transferring the patterns and lettering onto muslin or light fabrics, use a disappearing fabric-ink pen and place pattern on light-box or window to trace. For dark fabrics, transfer pattern lettering, using appropriate colored graphite paper.

For pattern pieces requiring machine-sewing, add ¼" seam allowance around all edges while cutting.

General Quilting Techniques

• Press fabric before using.

• Add ¼" seam allowances to quilt piece.

• Iron the ¼" seam allowances to one side, alternating sides between each square. Iron preferably toward the darker colored piece to prevent the seam from showing through a lighter piece.

• Use rotary cutter with a self-healing cutting mat to smoothly cut designs.

• Use embroidery hoops as needed.

Stitching Techniques

Backstitch (BS)

Bring needle up at 1. Go down at 2. Come up at 3. Go down at 1.

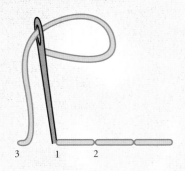

Blanket Stitch (BLS)

Bring needle up at 1. Go down at 2. Come up at 3, looping thread under needle. Continue for length of stitching, keeping needle vertical.

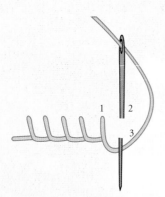

Cross-stitch (XS)

Bring needle up at 1. Go down at 2. Come up at 3. Go down at 4. To create another "X", bring needle up at 5, etc. All top stitches should lie in the same direction.

French Knot (FK)

Bring needle up at 1, using one strand of embroidery floss. Loosely wrap floss once around needle. Go down at 2, next to 1. Pull floss taut as needle is pushed down through fabric. Carry floss across back of work between knots.

Running Stitch (RS)

Bring needle up at 1. Go down at 2, creating a line of Straight Stitches with an unstitched area between each stitch.

Satin Stitch (SS)

Bring needle up at 1. Go down at 2, forming a Straight Stitch. Bring needle up at 3. Go down at 4, forming another smooth Straight Stitch next to the first. Repeat to fill design area.

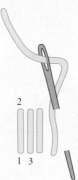

Straight Stitch (STS)

This stitch may be taut or loose, depending on desired effect. Bring needle up at 1. Go down at 2 upon achieving desired length.

Whipstitch (WS)

Bring needle up at 1. Whip thread over and go down at 2. Repeat until pattern has been established.

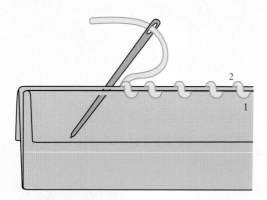

Alternative Stitches

Chain Stitch (CS)

Bring needle up at 1. Go down at 2, forming a loop—do not pull taut. Bring needle up at 3, catching the loop formed with the first stitch. Go down at 4, forming a second loop. Repeat.

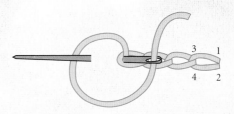

Feather Stitch (FS)

Bring needle up at 1. Go down at 2 and immediately back up at 3 on an angle, catching the loose loop just formed. Go down at 4. Bring needle up at 5 on the opposing angle, catching the loop just formed. Repeat.

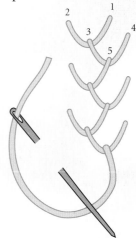

Warming
Up the
Hearth

MERRy

Star Ornaments

A very simple project, but a fun color-ful addition to any tree. These would also be great placed throughout a garland or on gift packages with the recipients' names stitched in the center.

Supplies

• General Supplies on page 12

• DMC embroidery flosses:
  489 red
  500 green

• White felt

Other ideas

With the addition of red felt for the two large snowflakes, I used the same materials to make this small tree skirt. Simply cut skirt to desired size, SS snow-flakes, and BLS edges. Adhere large snowflakes with fabric glue, then appliqué with a few stitches at center.

Here's How

1. Photocopy Star Ornaments patterns on page 96 and cut two per star from the felt. Refer to Using Patterns on page 13, transfer lettering onto muslin, using disappearing fabric-ink pen.

2. To stitch, use two strands floss.
   a. Plain stars: Using BLS with 489, stitch front onto back around ornament edges. Use six strands 489 for the hanger.

   b. Lettered stars: Using lettering patterns on page 96, transfer lettering onto stars. Using BS with 489, stitch lettering. Using BLS with 489, stitch around ornament edges, stitching front star onto back star.

   c. Tree stars: Using BS with 500, stitch triangular tree pattern. Using STS with 489, stitch garland. Using STS with 500, stitch stacked tree pattern. Using FK with 489, stitch the ornaments. Using BLS with 489, then stitch around ornament edges, stitch star front onto star back.

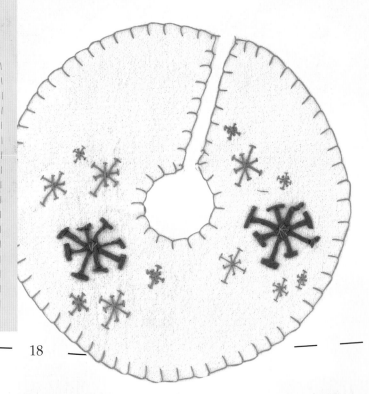

Snowman Stocking

On this project, I used a lot of buttons. In choosing the buttons, I tried to make certain that they were similar in color with the exception of the ones on the snowman. I wanted those to stand out.

Supplies

• General Supplies on page 12

• (29) Assorted 4-hole buttons

• Black acrylic paint

• Black wool (hat)

• Cotton batting (hanger, stocking pieces)

• DMC pearl cotton: #5 ecru, #8 black

• Fabric glue

• Faux fur (mittens, snowballs, and snowman body)

• Homespun fabrics or flannel (hanger, heel, mitten and stocking cuffs, stocking pieces, toe)

• Stylus

Here's How

1. Photocopy Basic Stocking patterns on pages 97–99 and Snowman Stocking patterns on page 100. Cut from appropriate fabrics. Refer to Using Patterns on page 13.

2. Following directions on fusible webbing, adhere cuff, heel, and toe onto stocking front, and cuff onto stocking back.

3. Glue cuffs onto mittens. Let dry.

4. Using photograph on page 21 as a guide and RS with #5, stitch snowman and mittens onto stocking front. Using RS with #8, stitch hat. Using XS with matching thread, stitch buttons. Glue snowballs into place and let dry.

5. Layer stocking front and back onto cotton batting. Using RS with #8, stitch stocking tops, then RS around outer edges, leaving top open.

6. To make hanger, use fusible webbing and adhere fabric onto cotton batting. Stitch inside edge of fabric, using RS with #8. Stitch hanger ends onto front and back of stocking, using buttons and #5.

7. Using stylus and paint, dot eyes, nose, and mouth. Let dry.

Tip

The type of fabric and trims you use will determine the style of your project. For a chicer look, try using jewel-colored fabrics, accenting with beads, and using a hand-dyed silk ribbon for hanging.

Saying Ornaments

These ornaments could be hung from a peg rack, over a doorknob, in a wreath, etc. Fill with cinnamon-scented rose hips instead of polyester stuffing to give as party favors or neighbor gifts.

Supplies

• General Supplies on page 12

• (4) Small buttons

• DMC #8 black pearl cotton

• Homespun fabric or flannel pieces, 4"x5" (two per ornament)

• Muslin, homespun fabric, or solid piece 2"x2¾" (one per ornament)

• Polyester stuffing

• Variegated olive/rust ruffle-edged ribbon, ¼" wide

Here's How

1. Photocopy Saying Ornaments patterns on page 100. Referring to Using Patterns on page 13, transfer lettering onto muslin, using disappearing fabric-ink pen.

2. Using BS with one strand #8, stitch lettering onto muslin. Use FK to dot the "i."

3. Using BLS with one strand #8, center and stitch muslin onto one homespun fabric piece.

4. Machine-sew 4"x5" fabric pieces with right sides together, leaving small opening at bottom for stuffing.

5. Turn right side out and fill with stuffing to desired fullness. Use WS with matching thread to close opening.

6. Cut desired length from ¼"-wide ribbon for hanger.

7. Referring to photograph on page 23 as a guide, stitch buttons onto ribbon ends with #8, then stitch onto ornament corners.

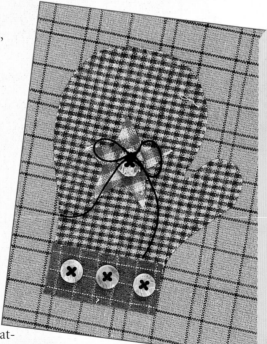

Other ideas

This appliquéd glove design could be made into an ornament, pillow, or picture. Simply cut pieces from desired fabrics and apply with fusible webbing. Stitch a few buttons into place to give dimension. Leave extra thread and tie a bow on top.

Santa Stocking

What makes this stocking so great is the full beard. Don't hesitate to use a lot of the wool. The thicker, the better.

Supplies

- General Supplies on page 12
- (9) Assorted large buttons
- Black acrylic paint
- Cotton batting (hanger, stocking pieces)
- DMC pearl cotton: #5 ecru, #8 black
- English-wool craft hair (beard)
- Faux fur (hat cuff)
- Homespun fabrics or flannel (cuffs, hanger, heel, stocking pieces, toe)
- Muslin (face)
- Stylus

Here's How

1. Photocopy Basic Stocking patterns on pages 97–99 and Santa Stocking patterns on page 101. Refer to Using Patterns on page 13. Referring to photograph on page 25 as a guide, cut out all pattern pieces from appropriate fabrics.

2. Following directions on the fusible webbing package, adhere heel, toe, and head onto stocking front and cuffs onto front and back. Using RS with #8, stitch along inside edges only of heel and toe, and bottom only of cuffs.

3. Using photograph as a guide, place and stitch buttons with #8.

4. With right sides together, fold hat in half and machine-stitch down side and top edge. Turn right side out and WS button closed. Stitch hat bottom onto top of Santa face. Gather hat a little over halfway to top and tie with #8. Stitch button in place.

5. Using RS with #5, stitch cuff onto hat.

6. Tightly stitch wool craft hair onto face for beard with #5, layering from neck to nose.

7. Layer stocking front and back onto cotton batting. Using RS with #8, stitch stocking tops, then RS around outer edges, leaving top open.

8. To make hanger, use fusible webbing and adhere fabric onto cotton batting. Stitch inside edge of fabric, using RS with #8. Stitch hanger ends onto front and back of stocking, using buttons and #8.

9. Using stylus and paint, dot eyes and let dry.

Snow Doll

How cute this Snow Doll would be, hanging by the front door to greet holiday guests! Her pockets can be filled with a variety of different items: candy canes, stars, Santas, or teddy bears. Her skates are purchased ornaments. Baby shoes or boots would work as well.

Supplies

- General Supplies on page 12

- (2) Ice-skating boots

- (2) Medium buttons

- (2) Twigs, approximately 6" long (arms)

- (6) Large buttons

- DMC pearl cotton: #5 ecru, #8 black

- Fabric glue

- Homespun fabrics

- Jute

- Large-eyed needle

- Muslin

- Ornament (for pocket)

- Polyester stuffing

- Small star button

Other ideas

Create this miniature Christmas stocking to display with your Snow Doll or use as an ornament. The basic stocking is made from cotton batting. Apply fabric pieces, using a simple RS with DMC #8.

Here's How

1. Photocopy Snow Doll patterns on pages 102–104. Refer to Using Patterns on page 13.

2. Referring to photograph on page 27 as a guide, cut out all pattern pieces from appropriate fabrics.

3. Machine-sew body front onto back with right sides together, leaving openings as to allow for stuffing.

4. Fold and sew right sides of each leg together, leaving top open for stuffing.

5. Turn all pieces right side out and fill with stuffing.

6. Insert legs into body opening and stitch closed. Make certain feet are positioned forward.

7. Sew shirt pieces with right sides together, leaving neck, arm, and bottom open.

8. Turn shirt right side out.

9. Cut 5"x45" skirt ruffle from fabric.

10. Cut 2"x10" front panel strip from fabric. Fold in half lengthwise, right sides together. Sew along long edge. Turn right side out. Center on bodice, folding one end over neckline, and hand-stitch in place. Pin remaining end at center bottom of shirt front.

11. With right sides together, sew skirt ruffle onto bodice. Gather while stitching. Make certain remaining end of front panel is tucked in and stitched as well. Remove pin.

12. Evenly space and stitch four large buttons down front panel with #8, also stitching through bodice. Stitch small star button over top button.

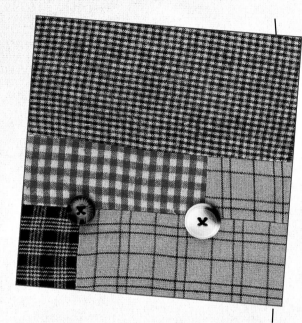

Optional Quilt Blocks

28

13. Using RS with #8, stitch two large buttons onto pockets and attach pockets onto bodice front. Leave top of pocket open.

14. Stitch one medium button onto each mitten front with #5, leaving excess pearl cotton to tie bow. Using BLS with #5, stitch mitten front onto back with wrong sides together, leaving wrist open.

15. Adhere mittens onto ends of twigs, using fabric glue. Wrap and glue cuff around top of mitten. Let dry.

16. Slip dress over head and onto doll. Insert twig arms through sleeves and deep into body, applying glue just before inserting into body. Glue openings in body closed around arms.

17. Slightly gather, tops of sleeves lengthwise toward shoulders and glue inside of shirt onto tops of twig arms. Let dry.

18. Gather-stitch with #5 around neckline to fit at neck.

19. Cut 1¼"x19" scarf from fabric. Cut narrow strips up from bottom edge on each end to make fringe.

20. Tie scarf around neck. Apply small amount of glue at knot in front to hold scarf in place.

21. For doll hair, cut 3" lengths from jute. Separate jute strands. Using one strand of jute and large-eyed needle, make one stitch at a time, centering each jute strand around outer edge of doll head, tying with a knot after each. Jute will naturally fray for the desired look.

22. Using pen, dot on eyes and draw a short straight line for nose.

23. Place ice skates on feet and ornament in pocket.

Other ideas

Below and on page 28 are several patterns that can be used as blocks for a small quilt to complement your doll. The fabric blocks can also be made smaller for the doll's pockets.

Santa Doll

The beard and the buckle was what I wanted to stand out on this doll, so I picked the biggest, flashiest button I could find and made the beard very long and thick.

Supplies

- General Supplies on page 12

- (3) Small gold bells

- Black fabric (boots)

- DMC #5 ecru pearl cotton

- English-wool craft hair (beard)

- Faux fur (boots, cuffs, hat, mittens)

- Large gold button

- Muslin (face)

- Polyester stuffing

- Red velvet fabric (body and hat)

- Tiny pearl beads

Here's How

1. Photocopy Santa Doll patterns on pages 105–106. Refer to Using Patterns on page 13.

2. Referring to photograph on page 31 as a guide, cut all pattern pieces from appropriate fabrics.

3. Sew body pieces with right sides together, leaving small opening at side of head for stuffing. Trim seam allowances.

4. Turn right side out through opening and fill with stuffing. WS to close opening.

5. Sew boot pieces with right sides together, leaving tops open. Trim and turn right side out.

6. Fill with stuffing. Tuck legs inside boots and stitch in place.

7. Using BLS, stitch mittens wrong sides together, leaving opening at wrist. Tuck arms inside mittens and stitch closed.

8. Place head onto body and WS around edge. *Note: Stitching will not show as the hat and beard will cover it.*

9. Tightly stitch hair onto face and sides of head, layering from neck to nose.

10. Sew sides and top of hat, right sides together, leaving bottom open to fit over head. Trim and turn right side out.

11. Stitch three bells on hat tip and stitch hat base around head.

12. Stitch cuffs around hat base and boots.

13. Stitch pearl beads around boot, mitten, and hat cuff. Stitch or glue large button onto center of tummy.

14. Dot eyes with marker.

Tip

For primitive Santa, use homespun plaid fabric for body and hat. Use buttons instead of pearl beads. See photograph on page 6.

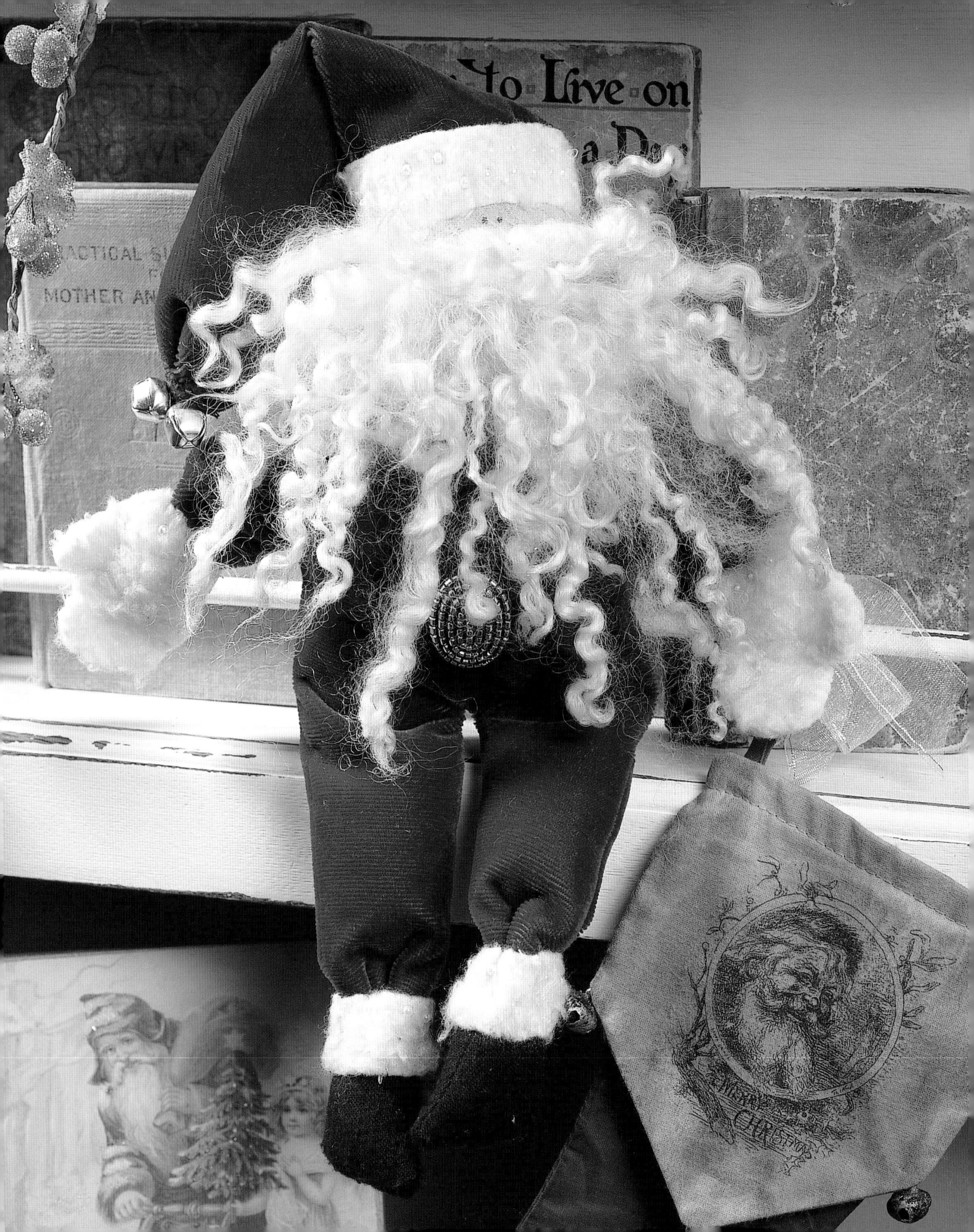
to Live on

Star Snowman Stocking

I purchased the star buttons for the mittens at a cross-stitch store; but you can find them, as well as the gingham buttons for the feet, at craft stores and scrapbook outlets.

Supplies

- General Supplies on page 12
- (2) Medium buttons
- (2) Star buttons
- (3) Small buttons
- (7) Large buttons
- Black acrylic paint
- Cotton batting (hanger, stocking pieces)
- DMC pearl cotton: #5 ecru, #8 black
- Fabric Glue
- Faux fur (mittens)
- Homespun fabrics or flannel (cuffs, hanger, hat, stocking pieces, toe)
- Tiny pearl beads
- Stylus
- White quilted fabric (star snowman)

Here's How

1. Photocopy Basic Stocking patterns on pages 97–99 and Star Snowman Stocking patterns on page 107. Cut from appropriate fabrics. Refer to Using Patterns on page 13.

2. Follow the directions on fusible webbing, adhere toe onto stocking front and cuffs onto front and back. Using RS with #8, stitch along inside edge only of toe, and bottom only of cuffs.

3. Place Star Snowman on front of stocking. Using RS with #5, stitch around edge of snowman, attaching to stocking front. Using stylus and paint, dot eyes.

4. To make snowman's hat, fold bottom of fabric up twice to make cuff. Using RS with #8, stitch along cuff. Fold sides to the back and WS edges together. Gather top and tie with #8. Place over star snowman head and glue into place.

5. Place mittens on hands and WS with #5.

6. Referring to photograph on page 33 as a guide, stitch all buttons. Use #8 for for stocking and #5 for snowman. Randomly place and stitch tiny pearl beads onto snowflakes.

7. Layer stocking front and back onto cotton batting. Using RS with #8, stitch around outer edges, leaving top open.

8. To make hanger, use fusible webbing and adhere fabric onto cotton batting. Stitch inside edge of fabric, using RS with #8. Stitch hanger ends onto front and back of stocking, using buttons and #8.

Christmas Tree Stocking

What I love about this socking is its simplicity. I hang all four stockings featured in this book along the front of an old pie safe in my dining room. Although I only use mine for decoration, they are big and sturdy enough to be filled to the brim with lots of surprises.

Supplies

• General Supplies on page 12

• (7) Rusty tin stars, 1⅛" tall

• (8) Assorted buttons

• Cotton batting (hanger)

• DMC #8 black pearl cotton

• Faux fur (stocking pieces)

• Hammer

• Homespun fabrics (cuffs, hanger, heel, toe, tree)

• Nail

Here's How

Note: If selecting a lighter weight fabric for the stocking, you will want to line the inside with cotton batting.

1. Photocopy Basic Stocking patterns on pages 97–99 and Christmas Tree Stocking patterns on page 108. Cut from appropriate fabrics. Refer to Using Patterns on page 13.

2. Using nail and hammer, pierce two holes in center of each star.

3. Using RS with #8, stitch inside edge of heel and toe, as well as top and bottom of cuff, onto front piece of stocking. Stitch top and bottom of cuff onto back piece of stocking.

4. Beginning with trunk, place and stitch tree onto stocking, using RS with #8.

5. Referring to photograph on page 35 as a guide, place and stitch stars onto tree. Using #8, stitch on buttons.

6. Place stocking front and back, wrong sides together, and stitch outer edge, using RS with #8.

7. To make hanger, use fusible webbing and adhere fabric onto cotton batting. Stitch inside edge of fabric, using RS with #8 stitch hanger and ends onto front and back of stocking, using buttons and #8.

Tip

For a great neighbor or hostess gift, reduce the patterns and make the stockings in a smaller format. Fill with candy or nuts.

five

three

Spicy Delight

Table Runner

Pretty floral fabrics would make a great runner for spring. Just think how great fall colors would be as well.

Supplies

- General Supplies on page 12

- (13) Chenille pieces, 4½"x5½"

- (20) Homespun fabric pieces, 4½"x5½" (Four complementary patterns are suggested.)

- Backing fabric

- Cotton batting

- DMC #8 black pearl cotton

Here's How

1. Referring to photograph on page 39 as a guide, sew first row of three randomly chosen pieces, right sides together. Press all seam allowances.

2. Repeat for second row of three pieces and press.

3. Sew first and second rows, with right

sides together. Continue this process until 11 rows are completed.

4. Cut fabric backing and cotton batting the same size as finished piece. Layer front and back with right sides together, placing cotton batting on top.

5. Sew around outside edges, leaving one small end open. Turn right side out. Use a ruler to push out corners. Using WS with matching thread, stitch opening closed and press.

6. Using BLS with two strands #8, stitch around edge of runner.

Place Mat

Follow the instructions for the Table Runner, using three rows instead of 11.

Other ideas

By using the optional Table Runner pattern on page 109 and changing the number of star rows used, the quilt block at right could become a wall hanging, or a bed quilt for a child "with stars in her eyes!" Stitch around the stars and add a button or two.

Coasters

These coasters are a great addition to any table and match perfectly with the Table Runner and Place Mat on page 38.

Supplies

• General Supplies on page 12

• (4) Chenille fabric pieces, 4"x5¼"

• (4) Cotton batting pieces, 4"x5¼"

• (4) Homespun fabric pieces, 4"x5¼", complementary patterns

• DMC #8 black pearl cotton

Here's How

1. Layer and sew one piece each of batting, homespun fabric, and chenille fabric (homespun and chenille fabric right sides together). Leave a small opening.

2. Turn right side out. Use a ruler to push out corners. WS opening closed with matching thread and press.

3. Using BLS with two strands of #8, stitch around edge of coasters.

4. Repeat process for remaining coasters.

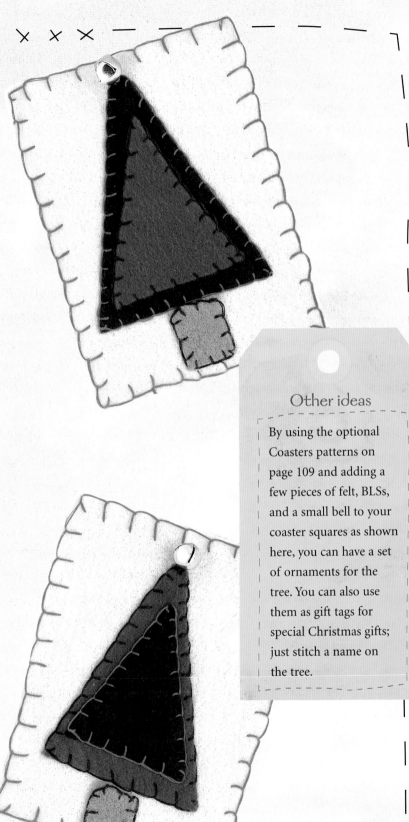

Other ideas

By using the optional Coasters patterns on page 109 and adding a few pieces of felt, BLSs, and a small bell to your coaster squares as shown here, you can have a set of ornaments for the tree. You can also use them as gift tags for special Christmas gifts; just stitch a name on the tree.

December
Dish Towel

What a great gift for your neighbors. You could add a plate of your favorite cookies and include the recipe.

Supplies

- General Supplies on page 12

- (2) Homespun fabric or flannel pieces, 1¼"x6" (scarf)

- (2) Small twigs (arms)

- (3) Black buttons

- Black felt piece, 4" square (boots)

- Cream flannel piece, 8" square (snowman)

- Dish towel

- DMC pearl cotton: #5 ecru, #8 black

- Fabric glue

- Hot-glue gun

Optional
Quilt Block

Here's How

1. Photocopy December Dish Towel patterns on page 110. Refer to Using Patterns on page 13.

2. Referring to photograph on page 43 as a guide, cut out all pattern pieces from appropriate fabrics.

3. Following instructions on fusible webbing, center and adhere snowman body onto dish towel, starting with largest circle at bottom. Leave room underneath for stitching the word "December."

4. Using BLS with #8, stitch around outer edge of snowman.

5. Stitch one end of each scarf piece onto sides of snowman's neck. Loop and tie in front.

6. Hot-glue twigs underneath the scarf.

7. Using XS with #5, stitch laces on boots, leaving extra thread to tie into a bow.

8. Adhere boots onto snowman with fabric glue.

9. Stitch buttons onto snowman's body.

10. Using FK with #8, stitch snowman's eyes.

11. Transfer December lettering underneath snowman at bottom of towel.

12. Using BS with #8, stitch "December."

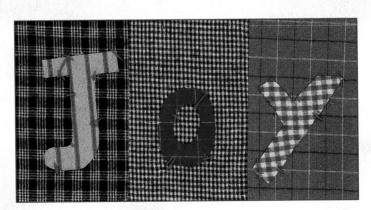

Christmas Advent Calendar

This calendar could be used year-round if a generic picture is used for the background and magnets are glued onto the back of each month's lettering.

When making the calendar, a different magnet for each day of the month can be added. Or all days of the entire month can be indicated, and one magnet, e.g. snowflake, small tree, star, snowman, etc., can be advanced as the days go by.

Supplies

• General Supplies on page 12

• (8) Circular tags, 1¼" diameter

• Decoupage medium

• Galvanized steel sheet

• Green acrylic paint

• Hammer

• Hot-glue gun or glue stick

• Ink pads: black, brown

• Nail

• Numbers: assorted scrapbook, stickers, Yahtzee, etc.

• Ribbons: 1½" wide (hanger)

• Rubber stamps: lettering, numbers

• Self-adhesive magnetic strips

• White cardstock

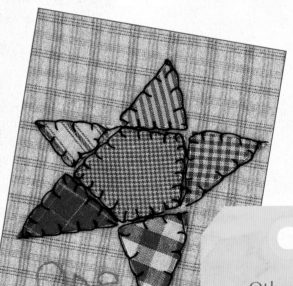

Other ideas

If you prefer the numbers for your advent calendar to be fabric, I have given a few examples at left on pages 46–47. Use combinations of fabrics and papers or numbered buttons; use your imagination and start counting!

DECEMBER
SUN MON TUE WED THU FRI SAT
TWO
#3
4
FIVE
Six
7
9
TEN
11
13
14
15
16
17
CHICAGO ILL DEC 18
19
20
21
22
23
24
25
26
27
28
ST. LOUIS DEC 29 9-30A 1905 MO.
30
31

Here's How

1. Photocopy Christmas Advent Calendar image on page 111 onto cardstock. Refer to Using Patterns on page 13.

2. Following instructions on decoupage medium package, adhere picture onto galvanized steel sheet. Let dry.

3. Roughly paint around edges to cover steel.

4. Cut cardstock into narrow strips to separate days of the month on calendar. Hot-glue strips onto image.

5. Stamp days of the week across the top with black ink.

6. Ink-dye circular tags and let dry. Refer to Using Walnut Ink Crystals on page 11. *Note: Prestained tags are available at a scrapbook outlets.*

Other ideas

Give a set of these hand-stitched numbers, at right and on page 47 as an early gift to count down from the beginning of the month or just the 12 days of Christmas. The personalized numbers will be appreciated by anyone. See optional Christmas Advent Calendar patterns on page 112.

7. Stamp the word "December" onto circular tags with black ink. Then lightly brush across top and edges with actual brown ink pad. Hot-glue into place.

8. Apply two coats decoupage medium, allowing to dry thoroughly between coats.

9. Adhere magnetic strips onto the backs of numbers and place accordingly. Refer to photograph on page 45 as a guide.

10. Using a large nail and hammer, pierce two holes at top of calendar and hang with ribbon, or adhere magnets onto back and hang on fridge.

Optional Numbers

Crazy-quilt Place Mats

Don't be concerned about this project being exact. The beauty of a crazy quilt is that it need not be perfect.

There is no set pattern for Crazy-quilt Place Mats. The pattern emerges as the place mat is built. Crazy-quilt pieces are attached together as you create the quilt.

Supplies

• Backing fabric piece, 12"x17"

• Cotton batting piece, 12"x17"

• DMC #8 black pearl cotton

• Fabric scraps, 14 complementary patterns

Here's How

Note: Referring to photograph on page 49 as a guide, begin the quilt in the top-left corner with a five-sided piece.

1. Build upon the first piece by working from one side to another. Each new piece is added by sewing right sides together along the edge of another piece, then flipping to the right.

2. Press seam allowances open and trim excess fabric. Most fabric pieces have four sides, while some may have only three. Once one side is finished, go back in the opposite direction until desired length and width is met.

3. Randomly stitch on the edge of crazy-quilt seams with variety of stitches, e.g. XS, BLS, RS, etc.

4. Once completed, place backing fabric and quilt top with right sides together. Place these on top of batting and trim to same size. Sew, leaving small opening. Turn fabrics right side out through opening. Batting will now be between fabrics. Press, then WS opening closed.

Other ideas

Not only could this additional quilt block idea be used as a place mat but also as a pillow, wall hanging, or a block in a larger quilt. Have each friend make a square and sign it, then assemble and give to a friend.

Merry Christmas

welcome

and to all a goodnight

Merry Christmas Tin

An option for the Merry Christmas Tin is to put family photographs in some of the compartments. With the exceptions of the candy cane ornament, fabric, ribbon, and star, items were purchased at a scrapbook outlet.

Supplies

• Fabric glue

• Fabric scraps

• Metal storage case, 5"x6½", containing twelve 1½"-diameter tins with clear lids

• Miscellaneous items: glitter, patterned paper, ribbons, stickers, trinkets, etc.

Here's How

1. Measure and cut fabric to fit inside top and bottom of storage tin.

2. Glue in place with fabric glue.

3. Referring to photograph on page 53 as a guide, decorate inside and out of each small tin with miscellaneous items.

4. Glue completed small tins in place.

5. Place and glue items inside front cover.

Other ideas

Hand-stitched fabric pieces such as the mitten above could be used inside the tins. Family members, names, words, symbols, all can be stitched and added to your tin. This optional Merry Christmas Tin pattern can be found on page 113.

Bulletin Board Mirror Frame

This is another project that can be changed seasonally. Simply remove foam-core board and cover with appropriate fabric for each season.

Supplies

• General Supplies on page 12

• Craft knife

• Double-sided artist's tape

• Fabric, cut 2" larger than mirror

• Foam-core board

• Light oak stain

• Old mirror with frame

• Paintbrush

• Sandpaper

• White satin finish latex paint

Here's How

1. Remove mirror panel from frame.

2. Clean frame and paint with two coats of white paint. Allow to dry thoroughly between coats.

3. Distress (sand) raised areas of the frame where aging would normally occur.

4. Apply stain lightly, quickly wiping off with soft cloth. Repeat process if desired.

5. Using craft knife, cut foam-core board to fit inside frame.

6. Cover foam-core board with fabric, stretching tightly. Secure with artist's tape.

7. Place and secure covered board in frame.

8. Decorate with ornaments, memos, etc.

Other ideas

Attach this star to the lower-right corner of the bulletin board, leaving inside edges of top and left points open to form a pocket. See the optional Bulletin Board Mirror Frame pattern on page 113.

Merry Christmas Picture

A favorite poem or artwork from a child or special friend could be used in place of the picture, giving something to be treasured.

Supplies

- General Supplies on page 12

- Double-sided artist's tape

- Fabric glue

- Foam-core board, 5"x7"

- Homespun fabric or flannel piece, 7"x9"

- Picture frame, 5"x7"

- White cardstock

- White lace piece, approximately ⅝"x13"

Here's How

1. Use a vintage postcard or photocopy a Merry Christmas Picture postcard image shown on page 114. Mount onto cardstock. Refer to Using Patterns on page 13. Cut out postcard.

2. Center 5"x7" foam-core board on wrong side of fabric. Pull fabric edges to back of board. Secure with artist's tape.

3. Center and glue postcard onto front side of fabric.

4. Glue lace around edges of card.

5. Frame without glass.

Other ideas

Picture or pillow, this project idea is simply fun. Cut out desired color felt, then place and stitch onto fabric with a variety of stitches. Use FK for the ornaments, SS for the garland, and BS for the lettering. Apply fabric glue to secure edges. See the optional Merry Christmas Picture pattern on page 114.

Seasons Wall Quilt

This quilt would look great draped over the back of a couch, across the foot of a bed, placed on a tabletop, or used as a lap throw. Here again, don't be concerned about being exact. This quilt is primitive folk art.

Supplies

• General Supplies on page 12

• (2) Star buttons

• (5) Tiny buttons

• (25) Large buttons

• DMC #8 black pearl cotton

• DMC embroidery flosses:
    336 blue
    498 red
    838 brown
    890 green
    947 orange
    3345 green
    3362 green

• Duck cloth, 33"x34" preshrunk (backing)

• Homespun fabrics

• Muslin

Here's How

1. If desired, tea-dye any of the fabrics. Refer to Using Tea on page 11.

2. Photocopy Seasons Wall Quilt patterns on pages 115–117 onto muslin pieces. Transfer and cut all pattern pieces from appropriate fabrics. Refer to Using Patterns on page 13.

3. Stitch each pattern as follows:
   a. Be Mine: Using BS with 498, stitch heart. Using BS with #8, stitch lettering.

   b. Showers Bring Flowers: Using BS with 3345, stitch leaves and stems. Using BS with #8, stitch lettering. Stitch a small star, then a round button on top of the star to make a flower head. Repeat for one more flower. Finish flower heads by stitching round buttons into place.

   c. USA: Using BS with 838, stitch pole. Using BS with 498, stitch stripes. Using XS with 336, stitch stars. Using BS with #8, stitch lettering.

   d. Harvest: Using BS with 947, stitch pumpkin. Using BS with 3362, stitch stem and vine. Using BS with #8, stitch lettering

   e. Merry Christmas Tree: Using BS with 890, stitch trunk and branches. Using FK with 498, stitch berries. Using BS with #8, stitch lettering.

4. Sew individual quilt blocks together as follows:
   a. For Row 1
   Block 1
   i.   Cut one 5½" square block from desired fabric.
   Block 2
   i.   Trim "Be Mine" embroidery block to 5½"x4¾".

ii. Cut four strips from complementary fabrics:

        (a) 1¾"x5½"

        (b) 2½"x6"

        (c) 1½"x7½"

        (d) 2½"x7"

    iii. Sew strips around block, starting with (a) at top and working clockwise.

Block 3

    i. Cut one 7½"x7" block from desired fabric.

Block 4

    i. Cut five strips from complementary fabrics:

        (a) 2¼"x6"

        (b) 2¼"x6"

        (c) 1¾"x6"

        (d) 1¾"x6"

        (e) 1"x6"

    ii. Sew strips together along 6" edges starting with (a).

    iii. Sew four blocks together, from left to right, to form the first row. Set aside.

b. For Row 2

Block 1

    i. Trim "Showers Bring Flowers" embroidery block to 5" square.

    ii. Cut four strips from complementary fabrics:

        (a) 2½"x5"

        (b) 2½"x 7"

        (c) 1½"x 7"

        (d) 1½"x 8"

    iii. Sew strips around block, starting with (a) at right side and working clockwise.

Block 2

    i. Cut four strips from complementary fabrics:

        (a) 1¼"x7½"

        (b) 2½"x7½"

        (c) 1¾"x7½"

        (d) 1"x7½"

    ii. Sew strips together along 7½" edges, starting with (a).

Other ideas

You can easily make the quilt pictured on page 59 for any season of the year. Use the above quilt block (or the optional blocks on pages 61–62) as an idea and add your favorite artwork and sayings. If a quilt is too big of a project, make pillows or frame one square for each season.

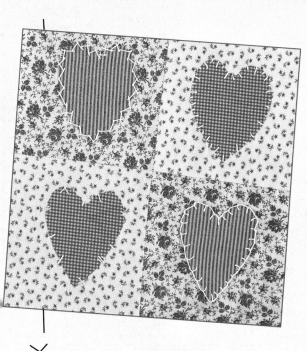

Block 3

i. Trim "USA" embroidered block to 4½"x5".

ii. Cut four strips from complementary fabrics:
   (a) 1½"x5"
   (b) 2¼"x5½"
   (c) 2½"x7"
   (d) 1½"x7½"

iii. Sew strips around block, starting with (a) at right side and working counterclockwise.

Block 4

i. Cut one 5½"x8" block from desired fabric.

ii. Sew four blocks together, from left to right, to form the second row. Set aside.

c. For Row 3

Block 1

i. Cut one 7"x7½" block from desired fabric.

Block 2

i. Cut one 7"x7½" block from desired fabric.

Block 3

i. Cut five strips from complementary fabrics:
   (a) 1¾"x7"
   (b) 2"x7"
   (c) 2"x7"
   (d) 2"x7"
   (e) 1¾"x7"

ii. Sew strips together along 7" edges, starting with (a).

Block 4

i. Trim "Harvest" embroidered block to 5" square.

ii. Cut four strips from complementary fabrics:
   (a) 1¾"x5"
   (b) 1¾"x6¼"
   (c) 1¾"x6¼"
   (d) 1¾"x7½"

iii. Sew strips around block, starting with (a) at top and working clockwise.

iv. Sew four blocks together, from left to right, to form the third row. Set aside.

Optional Quilt Blocks

d. For Row 4

Block 1

   i.   Trim "Merry Christmas" embroidered block to 4½" square.

  ii. Cut four strips from complementary fabrics:

     (a) 1½"x4½"

     (b) 2½"x5½"

     (c) 2"x6½"

     (d) 2"x7"

 iii. Sew strips around block, starting with (a) at bottom and working counterclockwise.

Block 2

   i.   Cut five strips from complementary fabrics:

     (a) 1½"x7½"

     (b) 2"x7½"

     (c) 2"x7½"

     (d) 2"x7½"

     (e) 1½"x7½"

  ii. Sew strips together along 7½" edges starting with (a).

Block 3

   i.   Cut one 7" square block from desired fabric.

Block 4

   i.   Cut one 6"x7" block from desired fabric.

  ii. Sew four blocks together, from left to right, to form the fourth row.

5. Sew four rows together, starting with Row 1 at top, to form the quilt center.

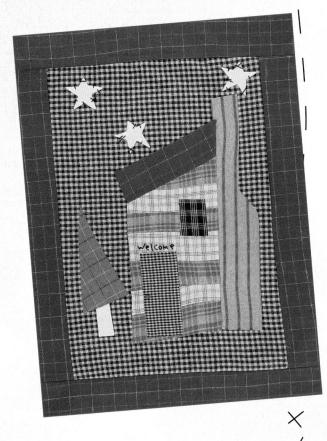

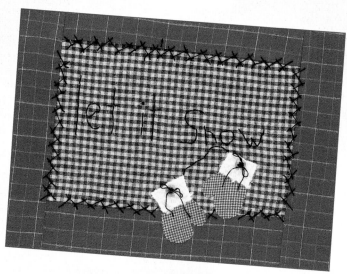

Optional Quilt Blocks

6. Sew quilt front together as follows:

a. For Inner Border

  i. Cut four strips from complementary fabrics:

    (a) 3"x28½"

    (b) 3"x30½"

    (c) 3"x31½"

    (d) 3"x32½"

  ii. Sew strips around the large four-row block, starting with (a) at bottom and working counterclockwise.

b. For Outer Border

  i. Cut four strips from complementary fabrics:

    (a) 2½"x30½"

    (b) 2½"x31"

    (c) 2½"x31½"

    (d) 2½"x32½"

  ii. Sew strips around border, starting with (a) at the left side and working clockwise.

7. With right sides together, sew duck cloth backing onto quilt front, leaving 4" opening along the bottom. Turn fabric right side out, using this opening.

8. WS opening closed with matching thread.

9. Using large buttons and several strands of pearl cotton, hand-stitch buttons on top at each square corner. Stitch through fabric backing as well to secure front onto back.

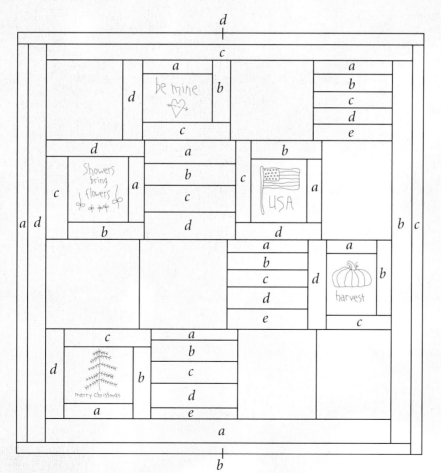

Placement Diagram

Jolly Christmas Picture

This project is so simple you could make one for each season or holiday. Merely change fabrics, frame colors, and pictures. It is also a great way to display loved ones' photographs.

Supplies

- General Supplies on page 12
- (2) Black photo corners or cardstock
- (2) Red 4-hole buttons
- DMC #8 black pearl cotton
- Double-sided artist's tape
- Fabric glue
- Foam-core board, 5"x7"
- Heavy cardstock
- Homespun fabric or flannel piece, 7"x9"
- Picture frame, 5"x7"

Here's How

1. Use a vintage postcard or photocopy the optional Jolly Christmas Picture image on page 118 onto heavy cardstock to make postcard. Refer to Using Patterns on page 13. Cut out postcard.

2. Press the fabric.

3. Center 5"x7" foam-core board on wrong side of fabric. Pull fabric edges to back of board. Secure with artist's tape.

4. Center and glue postcard onto front side of fabric.

5. Place and glue photo corners onto postcard.

6. Stitch Xs in button holes with #8.

7. Glue buttons onto photo corners.

8. Frame without glass.

Other ideas

Wool fabric scraps were used for the quilt square at right. Since any size of frame can be used, adjust the design to the size of the frame. Layer many fabrics for a dimensional look and add beads and buttons. See optional Jolly Christmas picture pattern on page 118.

Angel Pillow

To make the pillow larger in this project, either increase the width of the border fabric or add another row of border fabric.

Supplies

• (3) Tortoiseshell buttons, ⅜" wide

• DMC #8 black pearl cotton

• DMC embroidery flosses:
   420 taupe
   640 light brown
   729 straw
   977 gold
   3362 green
   3826 rust

• Fabric backing piece, 8½"x9"

• Hammer

• Homespun fabrics pieces: (2) 2"x9½", (2) 2"x8½", complementary patterns (borders)• Muslin piece, 5½"x8½"

• Nail

• Polyester stuffing

• Small metal star

Here's How

1. Tea-dye the muslin piece. Refer to Using Tea on page 11.

2. Photocopy Angel Pillow patterns on pages 119–121 and transfer onto the tea-dyed muslin piece. Refer to Using Patterns on page 13.

3. Sew 9½" borders, right sides together, onto tea-dyed muslin sides. Repeat with 8½" borders for top and bottom.

4. Use hammer and nail to pierce two holes into metal star, then stitch onto angel.

Other ideas

Using the optional Angel Pillow pattern on page 120, the star at left is very simple to make. It can be added to your pillow, made into square pillow ornaments filled with pine potpourri, or ironed onto craft paper and used to wrap your holiday presents. You might want to wrap empty presents and put them under the tree, each with a different color star and a different button.

5. To hand-stitch pillow, use three strands of floss.

    a.   Angel body and skirt outline: BS with 3362

    b.   Wings outline: BS with 640

    c.   Head outline: BS with 729

    d.   Eyes: FK with 420

    e.   Nose: SS with 420

    f.   Mouth: BS with 420

    g.   Hair: BS with 3826

    h.   Boots: BS with #8 (Use one strand.)

    i.   Boot laces: XS with #8 (Use one strand.)

    j.   Skirt inside edge: BS with 977;
         fill in: SS with 977

    k.   Stars inside wings: BS with 977

    l.   Star #1 & #2 outline: BS with 729

    m. Star #1 fill in: FK with 729

    n.   Star #2 fill in: BS with 729

    o.   Xs under the angel: XS with 3826

    p.   Angel lettering: BS with #8

    q.   Edge of muslin: RS with #8

    r.   Place and stitch buttons and star
         with 3362

6. Press seam allowances toward sides first, then toward top and bottom. *Note: Do not press fabric if a crinkled and aged look is desired.*

7. Sew backing onto front, with right sides together, leaving small opening. Turn right side out, using a small ruler to shape corners.

8. Fill to desired fullness with stuffing.

9. WS opening closed with matching floss.

Tip

Rather than making this project into a pillow, it can be placed in an 8"x10" frame without glass.

Optional Quilt Blocks
above and right

Snow Angel Picture

When picking out fabrics, remember to choose colors and patterns that appeal to you and go well in your home.

Supplies

- General Supplies on page 12

- (3) Tortoiseshell 4-hole buttons, ⅜" wide

- DMC embroidery flosses:
    - 420 light brown
    - 498 red
    - 742 gold
    - 840 light brown
    - 890 green
    - 3362 green
    - 3781 dark brown
    - 3826 rust

- DMC pearl cotton: #5 ecru, #8 black

- Foam-core board, 11"x12"

- Frame, 11"x12"

- Homespun fabric or flannel pieces: (2) 3"x8", (2) 3"x12" complementary patterns (borders)

- Muslin piece, 7"x8"

Here's How

1. Tea-dye the muslin piece. Refer to Using Tea on page 11.

2. Photocopy Snow Angel Picture pattern on page 122 and transfer onto tea-dyed muslin piece. Refer to Using Patterns on page 13.

3. Sew 3"x8" borders onto sides of muslin. Press seams toward outside edge. Do not press fabric if a crinkled and aged look is desired.

4. Sew 3"x12" borders onto top and bottom. Press seam allowances toward outside edges.

5. To hand-stitch picture, use three strands of floss.
    a. Angel dress: BS with 742
    b. Angel sleeves and skirt: BS with 890
    c. Angel gloves outline: BS with 498; inside: FK with 498
    d. Star on angel skirt: BS with 498
    e. Angel wings outline: BS with 3826 inside: XS with 3826
    f. Angel head: BS with #5
    g. Angel eyes: FK with 420
    h. Angel nose: SS with 3826
    i. Angel boots: BS with 3826
    j. Snowflakes: STS with #5
    k. Snow mounds: BS with #5
    l. Tree trunk and branches: BS with 840
    m. Leaves: STS with 3362
    n. Berries: FK with 498
    o. House frame and windows: BS with 420
    p. House roof: BS with 3781
    q. "Snow Angel" lettering: BS with #8 (Use two strands.)
    r. Edge: RS and XS #8 (Use two strands.)

Tip

To make this project into a pillow, simply cut backing fabric to same size as finished piece and follow Angel Pillow, Steps 7–9, on page 68.

6. Stitch buttons into place, referring to photograph above as a guide.

7. Frame without glass, using foam-core board as backing.

And to All a Good Night Picture

Each year I give my children and their families a Christmas book at the first of the season. Along with the book, I give something pertaining to the story. For example:

- *A Tale of Three Trees*:
  a set of miniature trees
- *A Snowman Named Bob*:
  a snowman doll
- *T'was the Night Before Christmas*:
  this project

Supplies

- General Supplies on page 12
- (5) metal-rimmed circular tags, 1½" diameter
- Black ink pad
- English-wool craft hair
- Gold ribbon, 1½" wide
- Hot-glue gun or glue stick
- Large shipping tag
- Picture frame, 8"x10"
- Rubber stamps, lettering
- Scrapbook paper or fabric
- Small white papier-mâché Christmas ornament
- Vintage image
- White cardstock
- White Christmas berries

Here's How

1. Photocopy And to All a Good Night Picture image on page 123 onto cardstock to make postcard. Refer to Using Patterns on page 13.

2. Cut scrapbook paper to fit frame back.

3. Refer to Using Walnut Ink Crystals on page 11 to prepare the shipping tag and circular tags. *Note: Prestained tags are available at a scrapbook outlet.*

4. Stamp the words, "And to All a Good" onto the shipping tag with black ink. Stamp each letter of "NIGHT" onto individual circular tags.

5. Cut a piece from ribbon and tie onto large shipping tag. Cut a piece from ribbon to run along bottom of picture.

6. Cut and thread wool craft hair through circular tag holes. Do not tie.

7. Using photograph on page 73 as guide, arrange postcard, ribbon, circular tags, shipping tag, and ornament onto background paper. When satisfied with placement, remove all except postcard.

8. Using glue-stick, adhere postcard.

9. Adhere ribbon along bottom.

10. Evenly space and hot-glue circular tags onto top of ribbon.

11. Using glue-stick, adhere large shipping tag into place. Hot-glue ends of ribbon in place. Tuck berries in ribbon knot.

12. Hot-glue ornament onto picture.

13. Frame without glass.

Bless This House Pillow

Not only is this a great Christmas project, it would also make a most-welcome housewarming gift.

Supplies

• General Supplies on page 12

• DMC #8 black pearl cotton

• DMC embroidery flosses:
  498 red
  646 gray brown
  729 straw
  742 gold
  781 golden bronze
  930 dark slate blue
  3021 brown
  3362 green

• Fabric backing piece, 16"x17½"

• Homespun fabric or flannel pieces: (2) 3½"x10", (2) 3½"x17½", complementary patterns (borders)

• Muslin, 11½"x10"

• Polyester stuffing

Tip
This block may be framed without glass and hung.

Here's How

1. If desired, tea-dye any of the fabrics. Referring to Using Tea on page 11, prepare muslin.

2. Photocopy and transfer the Bless This House Pillow pattern on page 124 onto tea-dyed muslin. Refer to Using Patterns on page 13.

3. Sew top and bottom border fabrics with right sides together onto muslin.

4. To hand-stitch the pillow, use three strands of floss.
   a. House frame and windows: BS with 646
   b. Roof: BS with 3021
   c. Tree trunk and branches: BS with 3021
   d. Angel face: BS with 3021
   e. Eyes: FK with 3021
   f. Leaves on branches: BS with 3362
   g. Door and chimney: BS with 498
   h. Doorknob: FK with 498
   i. Angel dress outline: BS with 498; inside: XS with 498
   j. Skirt: BS with 729
   k. Arms and legs: BS with 930
   l. Fence: BS with 781
   m. Moon and stars: BS with 742
   n. Border: RS and XS with #8 (Use one strand.)

5. Sew finished muslin piece onto backing, with right sides together. Leave a small opening to insert stuffing.

6. Turn right side out, using small ruler to shape corners.

7. Fill to desired fullness with stuffing.

8. WS opening closed with matching floss.

Peace Be Unto You Picture

If you have a favorite family photograph, copy it onto cardstock and use it in this project. This would make a great gift to family members if a photograph of a grandmother were used.

Supplies

• General Supplies on page 12

• (3) Metal-rimmed circular tags, 1½" diameter

• Black ink pad

• Gold ribbon, 1½" wide

• Hot-glue gun

• Large shipping tag

• Maroon ribbon, ¼" wide

• Picture frame, 8"x10"

• Rubber stamps, lettering

• Scrapbook paper or fabric

• White cardstock

Here's How

1. Photocopy Peace Be Unto You Picture images on page 125 onto cardstock. Refer to Using Patterns on page 13. Cut out images.

2. Cut background scrapbook paper to fit frame.

3. Refer to Using Walnut Ink Crystals on page 11 to prepare the shipping tag and circular tags.

4. Stamp the words, "PEACE BE UNTO" onto large shipping tag and the letters, "Y", "O", and "U" onto circular tags with the black ink.

5. Cut three 1" pieces from ¼"-wide ribbon. Knot each piece at center. Pulling one ribbon through each hole on circular tags, leaving knot on front of tag. Hot-glue end to back of tag.

6. Tie 1½"-wide ribbon on shipping tag.

7. Layer and arrange cards and tags on background paper to get an idea of placement. When satisfied with arrangement, remove all but bottom card. Hot-glue card into place.

8. Again, arrange cards and tags, layering and overlapping. Remove all but next bottom card. Hot-glue into place. Continue process until all cards are glued down, leaving printed shipping tag and circular tags until last.

9. Arrange circular tags and hot-glue into place. Leave ribbon ends loose.

10. Hot-glue large shipping tag into place. Hot-glue ends of 1½"-wide ribbon to edge of background scrapbook paper. This will be tucked under edge of frame. Play with and shape ribbon first to give depth and movement.

11. Frame without glass.

forever friends

Christmas Cheer

merry

be min

Keepsake Box

This is a lovely way to wrap a gift for someone, giving them two gifts in one. Treasures and mementos can be stored in such a box.

Supplies

- General Supplies on page 12

- Brown wire-edged ribbon, 1½" wide

- Fabric glue

- Papier-mâché box with lid

- Scrapbook paper, complementary patterns

Here's How

1. Measure and cut paper for box top and bottom with extra for overlap.

2. Following instructions on decoupage medium package, apply one coat to outside of box. Let dry. Decoupage and smooth paper, wrapping over inside edge and underneath edge. Apply another coat over top of paper. Let dry.

3. Repeat Step 2 above for bottom of box, then top of lid.

4. Cut two pieces from ribbon for bow on box lid, gluing one edge of each piece to side edge of lid. Let dry.

5. Repeat Step 2 for sides of lid.

6. Apply final coat over all paper pieces.

7. Tie ribbon into a bow.

Other ideas

This alternate project idea uses fabric instead of paper. Attach ribbon rosebuds, or whatever you like, to the lid with fabric glue. Then give this as a gift filled with something sentimental.

Merry Tree Gift Tag

This tag project would also be great used as an invitation to a Christmas party. Simply stamp date, time, and location. Other party instructions could be on the back side of the tag.

Supplies

• General Supplies on page 12

• Black ink pad

• Clear adhesive dots

• Corrugated scrapbook paper

• Craft glue

• Large shipping tag

• Ornament stickers

• Red ribbon, ¼" wide

• Red wire-ribbon cord

• Rubber stamps, lettering

Here's How

1. Dye shipping tag. Refer to Using Walnut Ink Crystals on page 11. *Note: Prestained tags are available at scrapbook outlets.*

2. Cut tree-shaped triangle from corrugated scrapbook paper to fit on tag.

3. String the ornaments by their hangers onto the cord while wrapping cord around corrugated tree. Affix each ornament to tree front with dots. Glue cord ends onto back of tree.

4. Glue tree onto tag.

5. Wrap ribbon around tag and tree. Glue ribbon ends onto back of tag.

6. Stamp the word "Merry" across bottom of tag with black ink.

7. Tie tag onto gift with cord and ribbon.

Other ideas

For fabric tags, stitch branches, trunk, and lettering with floss. Apply ornaments, star, and tree-base fabrics with fusible webbing to background fabric. Cut in rectangular tag shape. Punch a hole in the top.

Friendship Gift Frame

A favorite photograph of you and a friend can be placed into the Friendship Gift Frame. It can be given with the stamp box filled with postage stamps. (See Postage Stamp Gift Box on page 86.)

Supplies

• General Supplies on page 12

• Decoupage medium

• Vintage papers, postcards, stamps, or print fabrics

• Vintage text scrapbook paper

• Wooden picture frame

Here's How

1. Remove backing and glass from frame.

2. Following instructions on the decoupage medium package, adhere background scrapbook paper to front of frame. Let dry.

3. Place and adhere papers, postcards, and stamps. Let dry.

4. Apply final coat of decoupage medium and let dry thoroughly.

5. Replace glass and backing.

Other ideas

Small fabric postcard shapes can be used to cover a frame or to make a small pillow for a close friend. You can make the pillow minature, line it, and fill with holiday potpourri.

Postage Stamp Gift Box

Fill this box with stamps, tie with ribbon, and give as a gift to a college student, faraway friend, or family member. It is also perfect for jewelry or other mementos.

Supplies

• General Supplies on page 12

• Decoupage medium

• Postage-stamp stickers

• Postcard stickers or small pieces of fabric cut into postage-stamp shapes

• Small cardboard box with lid

Here's How

1. Affix postage-stamp stickers onto box lid, overlapping to cover entire lid.

2. Overlap and affix postcard stickers onto bottom and sides of box.

3. Following instructions on the decoupage medium package, apply one coat to lid and bottom. Let dry.

Other ideas

Give this pillow to someone you love. It is made with a few scraps of fabric, a piece of old lace, a decorative stitch, and the pieces from an old earing. This could also be filled with potpourri to make a sachet, or with sand to use as a paperweight.

Peace, Love, Joy Gift Tags

By simply replacing the snowflakes with red hearts, you have wonderful Valentine's Day cards. Stamp "to" and "from" on the back of tag, then give to your special Valentine.

Supplies

- General Supplies on page 12

- Black ink pad

- Cream ribbon, ¼" wide

- Fabric glue

- Fibers, various strands

- Rubber stamps, lettering

- Shipping tags: (1) small (Joy),
  (2) large (Peace and Love)

- Snowflake stickers

- White laces: ⅝" wide (Love),
  ⅜" wide (Joy), 1" wide (Peace)

Here's How

1. Dye shipping tags. Refer to Using Walnut Ink Crystals on page 11. *Note: Prestained tags are available at scrapbook outlets.*

2. Referring to photograph on page 89 as a guide, glue a piece of lace along bottom of tag. Wrap and glue ends onto back. *Note: Glue lace for "Love" tag diagonally.*

3. Stamp the word "Peace" with black ink on a tag. Repeat, stamping the words "Love" and "Joy" on the remaining tags.

4. Affix snowflake stickers onto tags.

5. Tie each tag with 3–4 strands of fibers.

Other ideas

For fabric tags, begin with cardstock tags, cover with fabric that has been embroidered, and attach lace with fabric glue. Rather than using these as gift tags, try using them to label your photograph boxes.

Oh, Holy Night Gift Tag

The copper wire is very pliable so when this project is complete, don't be afraid to play with it a little to give it dimension.

Supplies

- General Supplies on page 12

- Black ink pad

- Brown ribbon, ¼" wide

- Craft glue

- Gold ribbon, ½" wide

- Gold ultrafine glitter

- Large shipping tag

- Pencil

- Rubber stamps, lettering

- Small hole punch

- Star stickers

- String

- Thin copper wire

- Thin gold wire-ribbon cord

- Wire cutters

Here's How

1. Dye shipping tags. Refer to Using Walnut Ink Crystals on page 11. *Note: Prestained tags are available at scrapbook outlets.*

2. Stamp the words, "Oh, Holy Night" down left side of tag with black ink.

3. Cut desired length from wire. Referring to photograph on page 91 as a guide, wrap end of copper wire around pencil. Place wire on tag, leaving wire straight where stars are to be placed. In between star placement, wrap wire around pencil to curl.

4. Where stars are to be placed, punch two small holes in tag on each side of wire. Tie wire to tag with string, knotting in back.

5. Affix star stickers onto tag over tied wire.

6. With your finger, apply craft glue very lightly and randomly over face of tag then sprinkle gold glitter onto glue. Tap back of tag to remove excess.

7. Tie tag with wire-ribbon cord and ribbons.

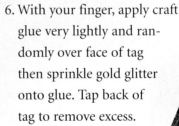

Journals

The ideas are endless for this project. Not only for design, but for uses of the journal. Add index tabs and you have an address book. Use floral paper or fabric to get a great gardening journal, use maps on the cover for a place to record the memories of a trip taken. Use your imagination.

Supplies

- General Supplies on page 12
- (2) Sheets scrapbook paper, complementary
- Black ink pad
- Bookplate
- Clear dot adhesive
- Composition journal
- Cream cardstock
- Fabric glue
- Glue stick
- Ribbon: ¼" wide (small journal), or ½" wide (large journal)
- Rubber stamps, lettering
- White lace

Here's How

1. Leaving spine uncovered, cut first sheet of scrapbook paper to size of book front cover plus 1" on top, bottom, and right-hand sides.

2. Using glue-stick, coat entire front cover and edges of book with glue.

3. Position scrapbook paper on front cover of book. Smooth paper completely.

4. Crease paper on the outer edges. Then starting at the corners, fold and glue excess paper to inside. Smooth completely.

5. Repeat Steps 1–4 for back cover.

6. Using fabric glue on right edge, adhere lace down edge of book spine, barely overlapping paper. Wrap ends over to the inside of cover and glue.

7. Using fabric glue, center and adhere a ribbon to the inside front and back covers for the tie.

8. Cut second scrapbook paper to fit inside front and back covers.

9. Using glue stick, adhere in place.

10. Using dot adhesive, glue bookplate to cover front.

11. Cut cardstock to fit bookplate, then stamp the word "JOURNAL" or another title, using black ink. Insert label into bookplate.

Tip

Journals are great gift ideas for friends and family. Personalize the journal with fabrics and trims that reflect the recipient's personality. On the first page of the journal, write about a special memory that you have of that person.

With
all kind thoughts
and Good Wishes for
Christmas and the Coming Year.

be mine

Showers bring flowers

STAMP

POST- CARD

PE ACE
BE UNTO

merry christmas

USA

Patterns
and
Images

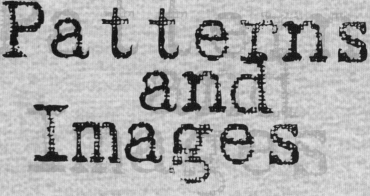

Christmas
Chimes
of Love,

harvest

Star Ornaments

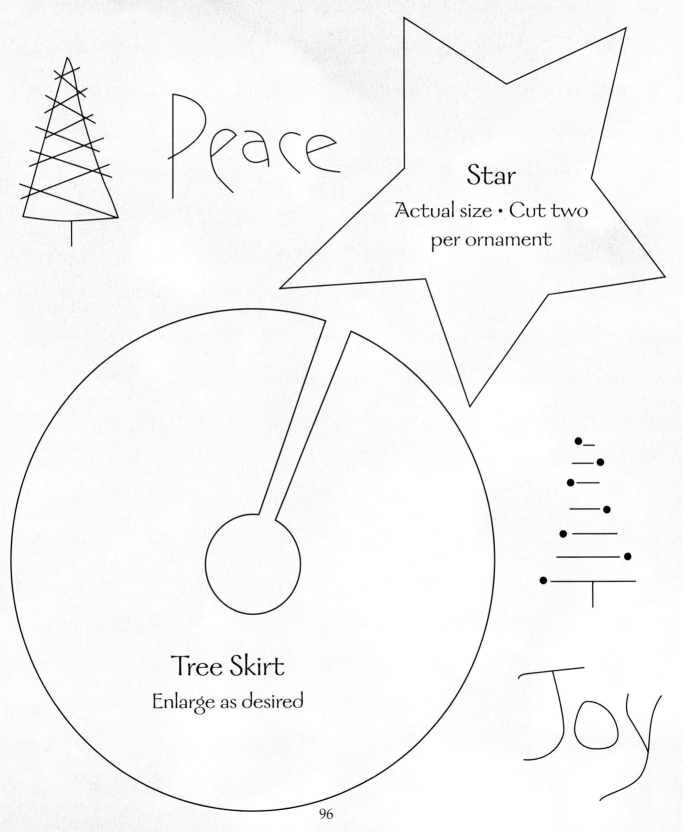

Peace

Star
Actual size • Cut two
per ornament

Tree Skirt
Enlarge as desired

Joy

Basic Stocking

Stocking Cuff

Actual size • Cut two

Hanger Front

Actual size • Cut one

continued on page 98

Basic Stocking

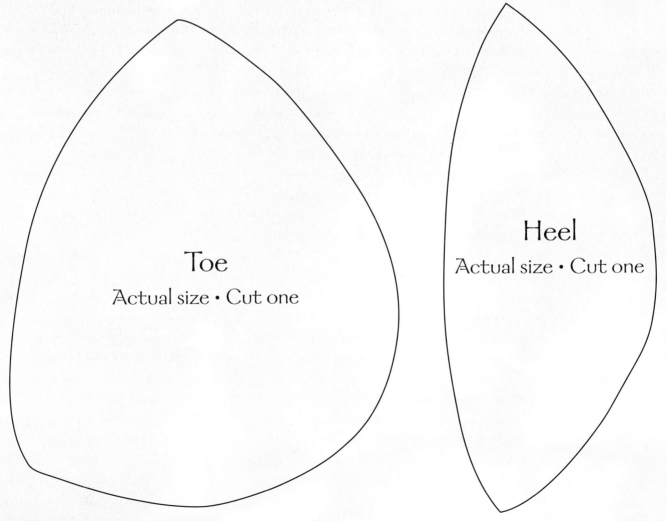

Hanger Back
Actual size • Cut one

Toe
Actual size • Cut one

Heel
Actual size • Cut one

Basic Stocking

Stocking

Enlarge 200% • Cut two from fabric
Cut two from batting
if instructions specify

Snowman Stocking

Mitten
Actual size
Cut four

Snowman Bottom
Actual size
Cut one

Snowman Torso
Actual size
Cut one

Snowman Head
Actual size
Cut one

Snowball
Actual size
Cut six

Saying Ornaments

Star
Actual size
Cut one

Mitten
Actual size • Cut one

let
it
Snow

merry

merry

merry

Santa Stocking

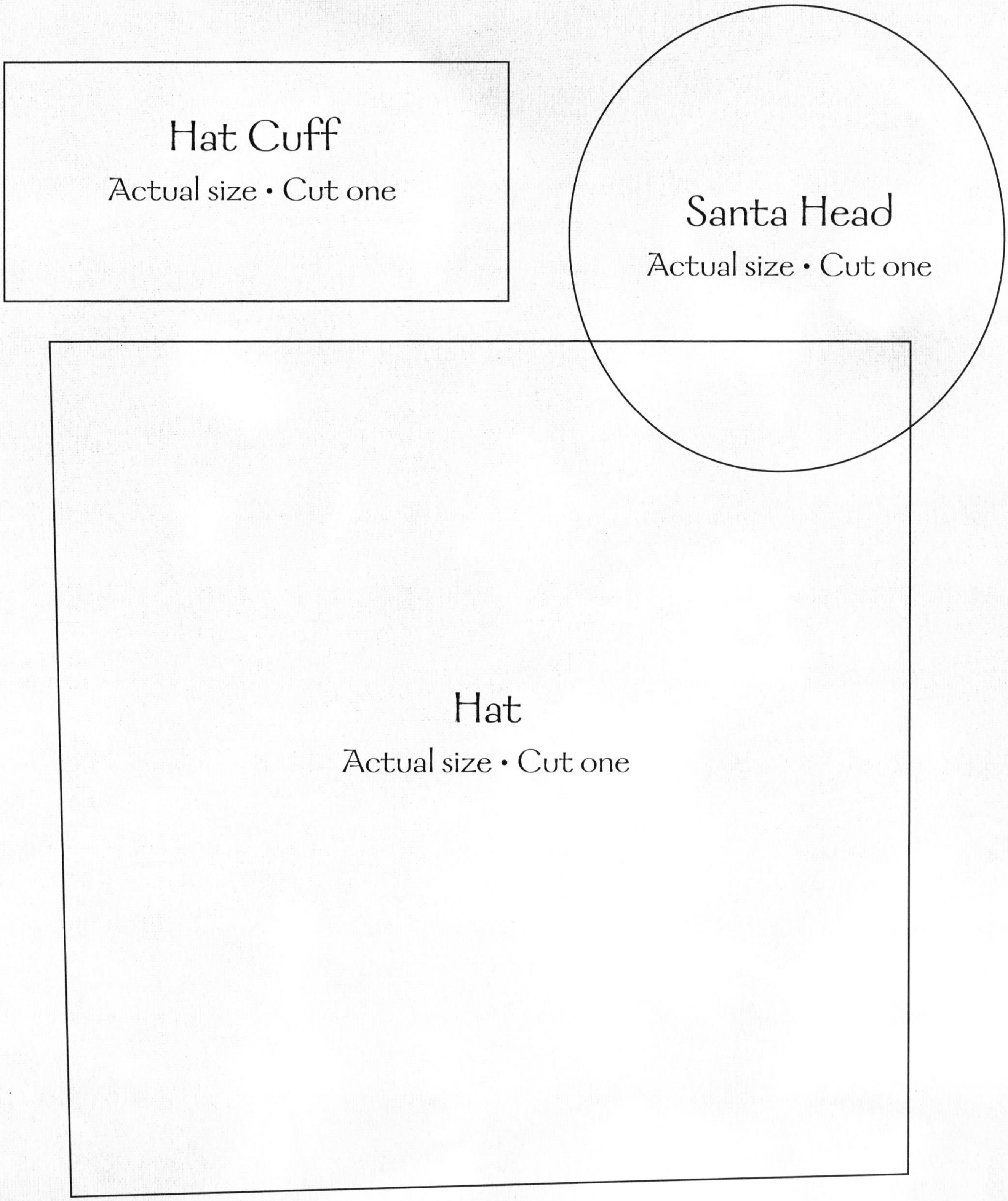

Hat Cuff

Actual size • Cut one

Santa Head

Actual size • Cut one

Hat

Actual size • Cut one

Snow Doll

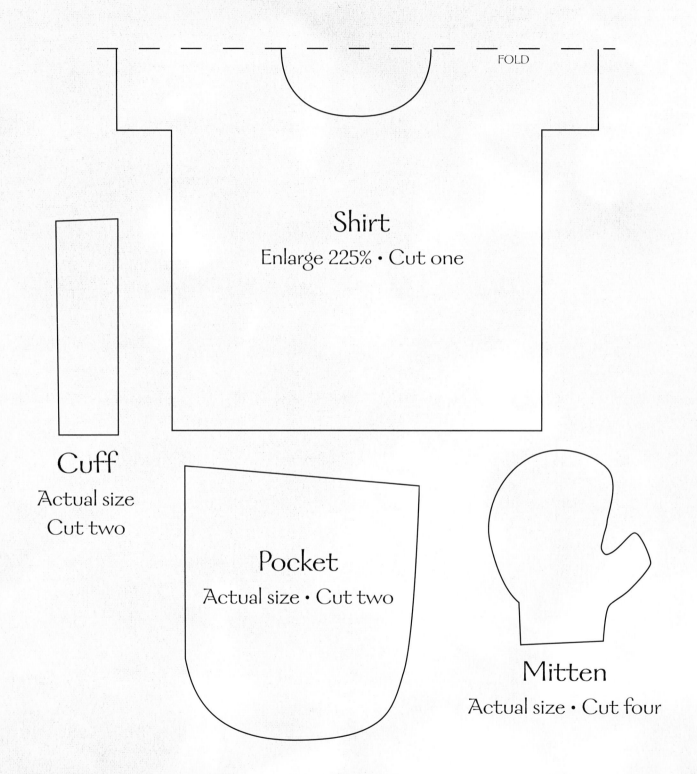

FOLD

Shirt
Enlarge 225% • Cut one

Cuff
Actual size
Cut two

Pocket
Actual size • Cut two

Mitten
Actual size • Cut four

Snow Doll

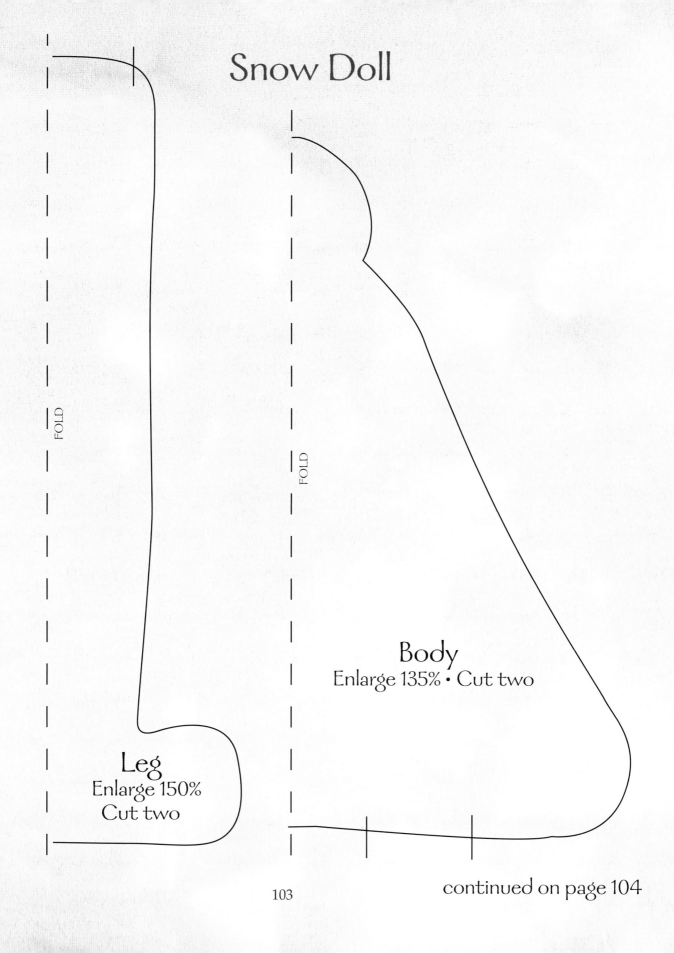

FOLD

FOLD

Leg
Enlarge 150%
Cut two

Body
Enlarge 135% • Cut two

103

continued on page 104

Snow Doll

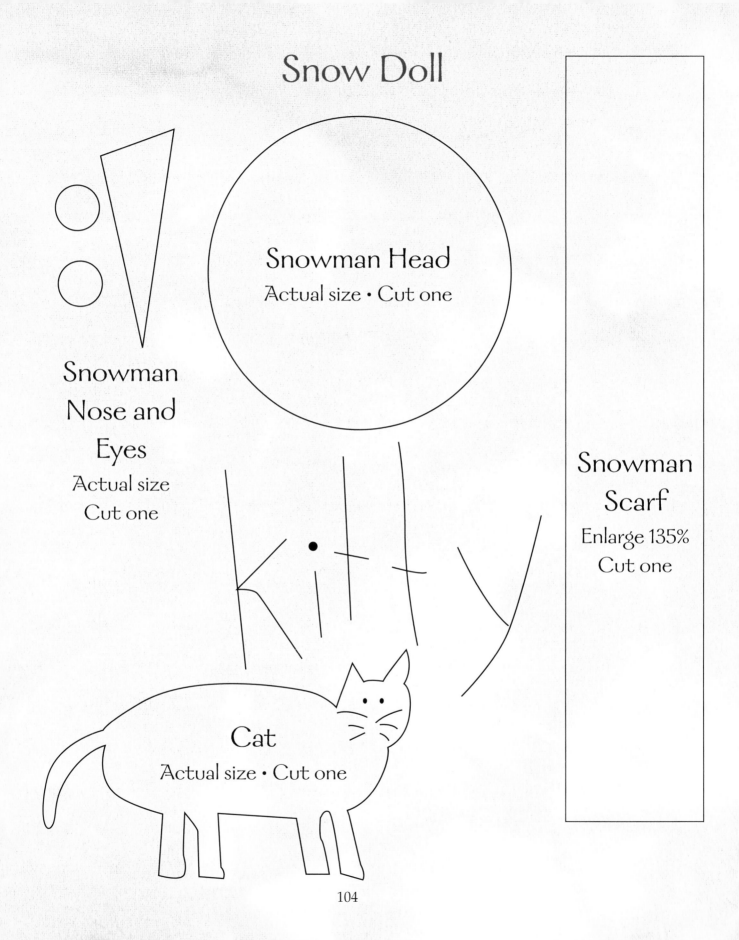

Snowman Nose and Eyes
Actual size
Cut one

Snowman Head
Actual size • Cut one

Snowman Scarf
Enlarge 135%
Cut one

kitty

Cat
Actual size • Cut one

Santa Doll

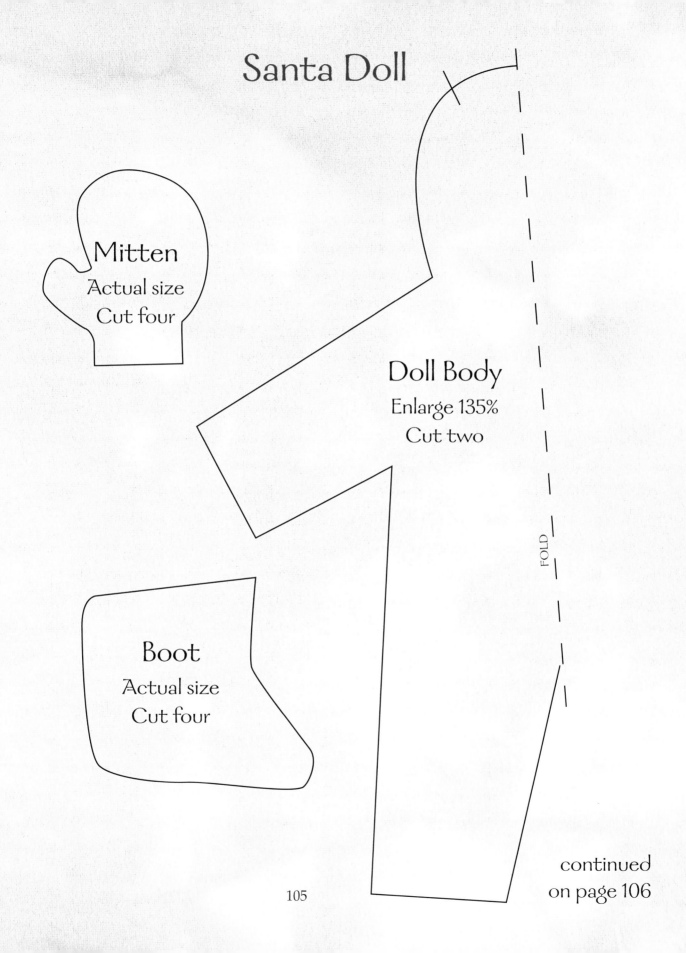

Mitten
Actual size
Cut four

Doll Body
Enlarge 135%
Cut two

FOLD

Boot
Actual size
Cut four

continued
on page 106

Santa Doll

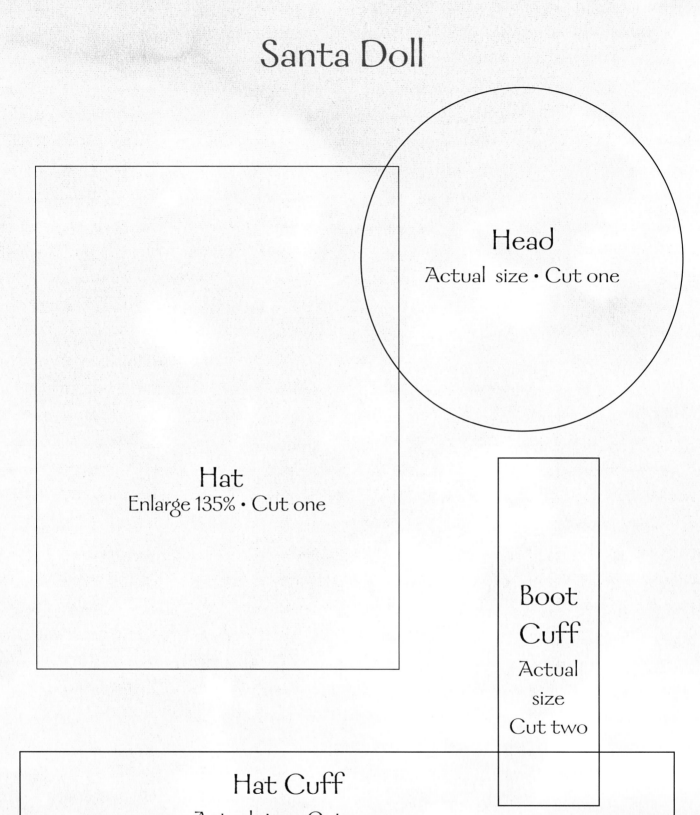

Head
Actual size • Cut one

Hat
Enlarge 135% • Cut one

Boot Cuff
Actual size
Cut two

Hat Cuff
Actual size • Cut one

Star Snowman Stocking

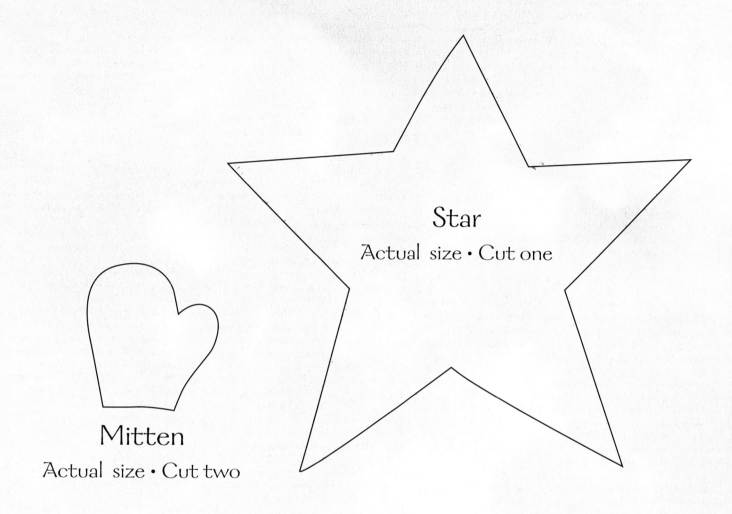

Star
Actual size • Cut one

Mitten
Actual size • Cut two

Hat
Actual size • Cut one

Christmas Tree Stocking

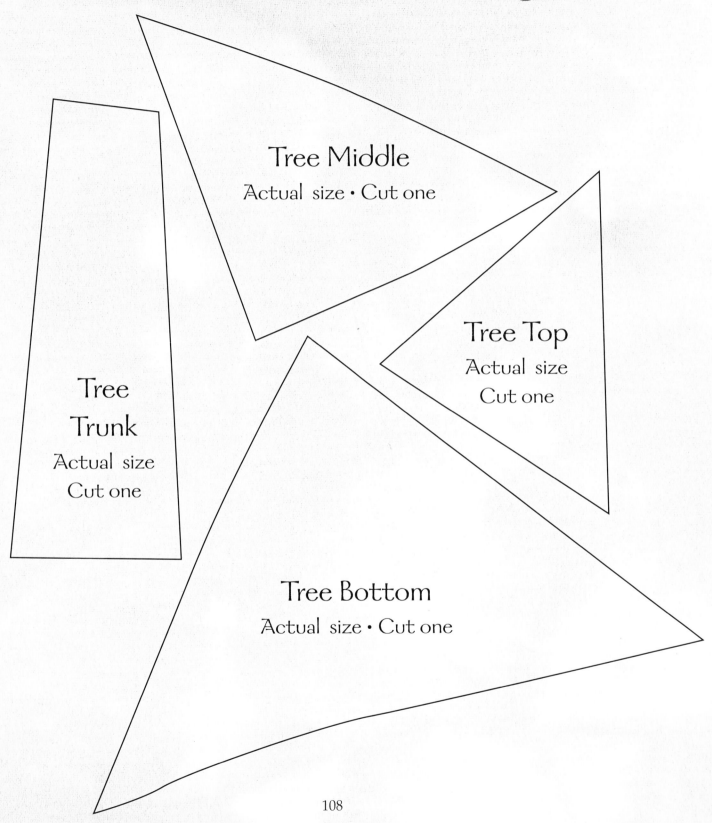

Tree Middle
Actual size • Cut one

Tree Top
Actual size
Cut one

Tree
Trunk
Actual size
Cut one

Tree Bottom
Actual size • Cut one

Table Runner

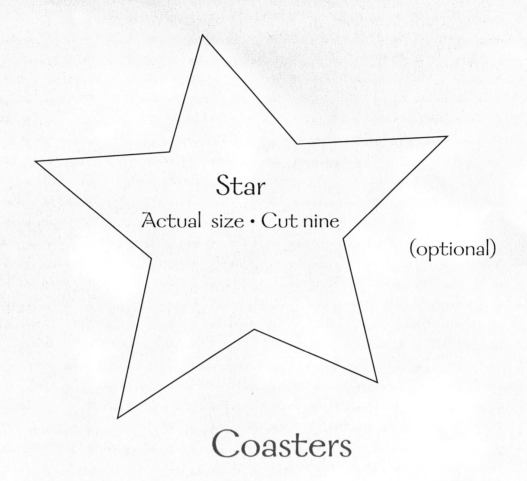

Star
Actual size • Cut nine

(optional)

Coasters

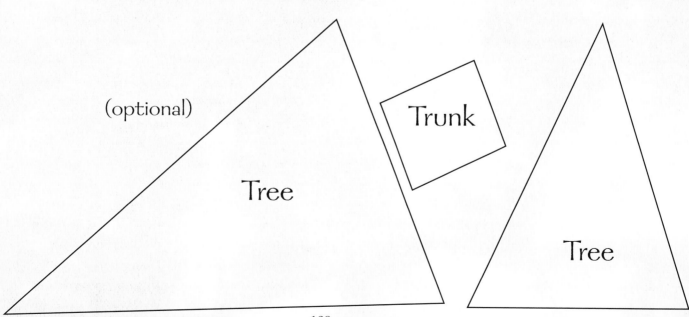

(optional)

Tree

Trunk

Tree

December Dish Towel

december

(optional)

Snowman Face
Actual size
Cut one

Snowman Torso
Actual size • Cut one

Snowman Bottom
Actual size • Cut one

Boot
Actual size
Cut two

Christmas Advent Calendar

continued on page 112

Christmas Advent Calendar

(optional star)

Six

five

three

Merry Christmas Tin

Note: Reduce to fit tin.

(optional images)

Bulletin Board
Mirror Frame

peace on earth

(optional)

Merry Christmas Picture

(optional)

(optional images)

Seasons Wall Quilt

merry christmas

(optional)

let it snow

(optional)

harvest

continued on page 116

Seasons Wall Quilt

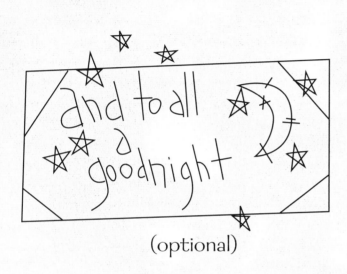

and to all a goodnight

(optional)

Showers bring flowers

Spring

(optional)

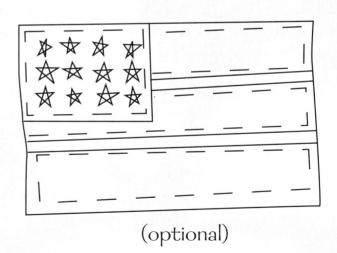

(optional)

Seasons Wall Quilt

be mine

USA

welcome

(optional)

Jolly Christmas Picture

(optional)

(optional image)

Angel Pillow

Enlarge 125%

continued on page 116

Angel Pillow

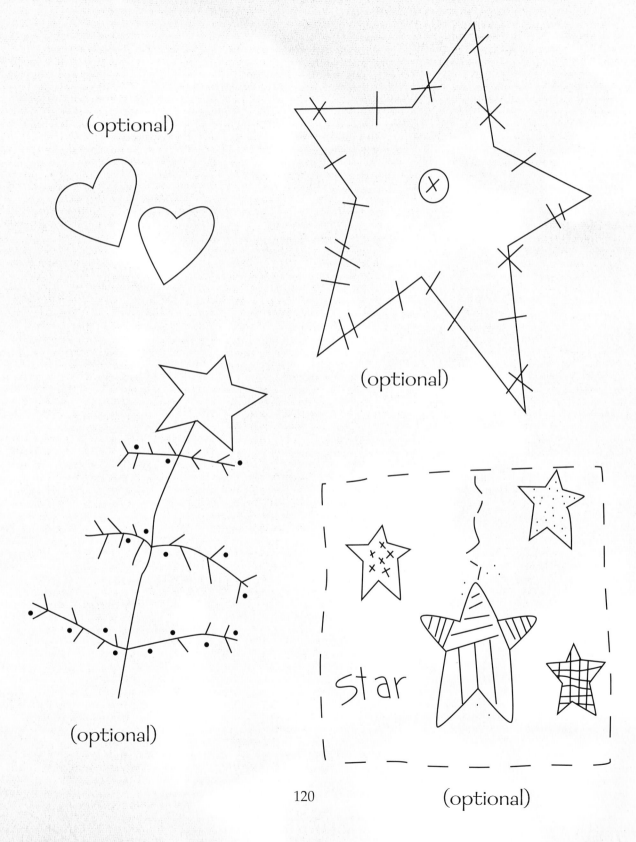

(optional)

(optional)

(optional)

star

(optional)

Angel Pillow

Christmas Cheer

(optional)

(optional)

Snow Angel Picture

Enlarge 125%

And to All a Good Night Picture

(optional)

All Images
Actual Size

(optional)

Bless This House Pillow

bless
this
house

Actual Size

Peace Be Unto You Picture

All Images Actual Size

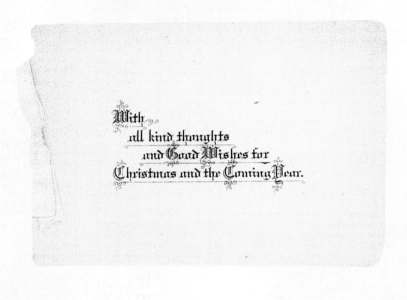

ACKNOWLEDGMENTS

This book is dedicated to my mother, Hanna Mae Delquadro Meacham. Your strength and loving kindness amaze me.

Thank-you to my children David, Heather, Chris, and Tyler, who cheer me on; my granddaughters Hanna and Hallie, who bring such joy to my life; Daniel, who makes my heart light; my sister Karen, who encourages me; and my dear friends Marcia and Debbie, whose loving help and support made it possible for me to accomplish *Quilted Projects for a Country Christmas*. Words cannot express how much you all mean to me. Much love! Once again, my heartfelt gratitude to Jo Packham— advisor, mentor, friend. I am most thankful.

To Scott and Kevin my photographers, and to all the behind-the-scenes staff at Chapelle, a heartfelt thanks for bringing this book to life.

• For further information, contact Hen Feathers by phone, 801-622-1866.